我想说谢谢
I am Thankful

著/谢莉 · 阿德蒙特

绘/穆罕默德 · 埃尔加

www.kidkiddos.com
Copyright ©2022 by KidKiddos Books Ltd.
support@kidkiddos.com

First edition

Translated from English by Luwan Han
译/韩璐湾

Library and Archives Canada Cataloguing in Publication
I am Thankful (Chinese English Bilingual Edition) / Shelley Admont
ISBN: 978-1-5259-7707-7 paperback
ISBN: 978-1-5259-7708-4 hardcover
ISBN: 978-1-5259-7706-0 eBook

Please note that the English and Chinese versions of the story have been written to be as close as possible. However, in some cases they differ in order to accommodate nuances and fluidity of each language.

灿烂的阳光透过窗户照进来，我睡醒了。

I wake up to the sun shining brightly through my window.

旁边躺着我最心爱的泰迪熊。

My favorite teddy bear lies next to me.

它是那么柔软、那么可爱，谢谢你，我的泰迪熊！

I am thankful for my teddy bear and for how soft and cuddly it is!

我伸伸懒腰，打个哈欠，慢悠悠地起床了。

I stretch and yawn, then slowly get out of my bed.

我聞到一股香香噴的味道從廚房飄來，闻起来像煎饼！

I smell something delicious coming from the kitchen.
It smells like pancakes!

妈妈做的早餐是世界上最美味的！感謝妈妈的廚藝⋯

My mom makes the best breakfast in the world! I am thankful for her cooking...

…特别要感谢她做的巧克力碎饼干。

…especially her chocolate chip cookies.

我跑到厨房里，看到妹妹已经在吃早餐了。

I run to the kitchen and I see that my little sister is already eating breakfast.

她笑着给我最热烈的拥抱，我感到非常快乐。我还是想说，感谢你，我的妹妹…

She smiles and gives me the biggest hug. It makes me happy. I am very thankful for my sister...

…尽管她有时有点烦人！

…even though she can be a little annoying sometimes!

今天，我要去参加我最好的朋友安娜的生日派对。

Today I am going to my best friend Anna's birthday party.

学校里的小伙伴们都会过去，到时一定特别好玩儿。

All my friends from school are going to be there. It will be lots of fun.

我该穿什麼呢？裙子，還是褲子？

**What should I wear?
A dress or pants?**

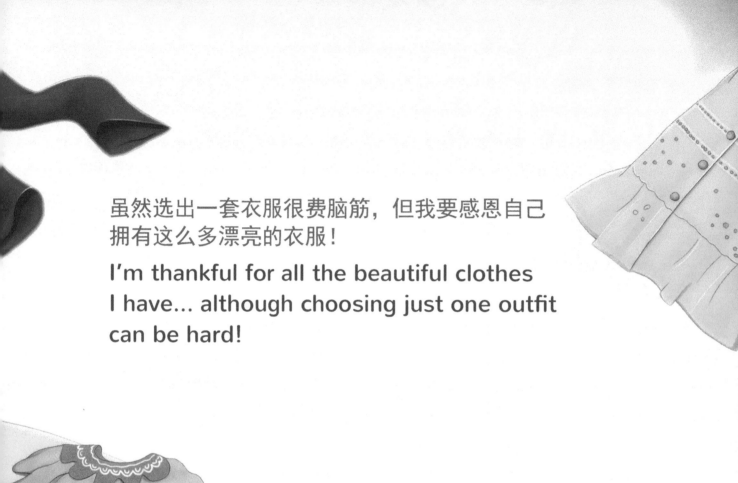

虽然选出一套衣服很费脑筋，但我要感恩自己拥有这么多漂亮的衣服！

I'm thankful for all the beautiful clothes I have... although choosing just one outfit can be hard!

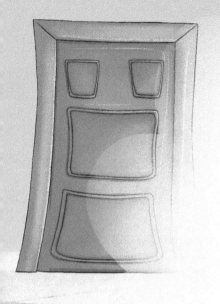

我来到派对，安娜向我跑过来。"你的裙子真好看！"她一边说，一边拥抱了我。

When I get to the party, Anna runs over. "What a lovely dress!" she says, and hugs me.

我很感恩，能有这样的好朋友。

I am thankful to have her as my best friend.

安娜的妈妈端出了生日蛋糕，它好大好大！做这么大的蛋糕，一定花了不少时间吧。

Anna's mom brings out her cake, and it's huge! It must have taken such a long time to make.

感谢这一切，漂亮的蛋糕、好玩的游戏…
I am thankful for the pretty cake, fun games...

…还有我的朋友们！

... and my friends.

我回到家时，妈妈为我准备好了洗澡水，里面是满满的泡泡。

When I get home my mom prepares a bath for me with lots of bubbles.

我玩起了泡泡，把它们放在下巴上，当作是胡子。这把妈妈给逗笑了。

I play with the bubbles and put them on my chin to make a beard. This makes my mom laugh.

感恩泡泡，它们让泡澡的时光如此愉快⋯

I am thankful for bubbles because they make bath time so much fun...

…但我更要感恩，妈妈的怀抱。

…but I am even more thankful for my mom's cuddles.

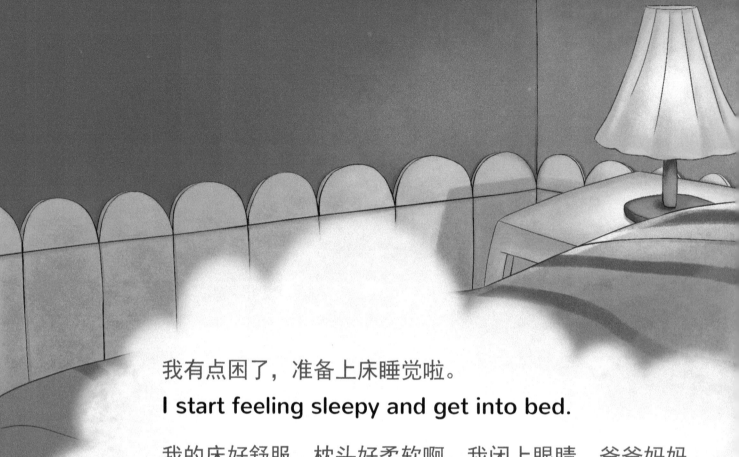

我有点困了，准备上床睡觉啦。

I start feeling sleepy and get into bed.

我的床好舒服，枕头好柔软啊。我闭上眼睛，爸爸妈妈给我留下了晚安吻。

My bed is cozy and my pillow is soft. My parents kiss me goodnight as I close my eyes.

感谢你们，我的家人。

I am thankful for my family.

最最感谢的，还是我最心爱的泰迪熊。

And most of all, I am thankful for my favorite teddy bear.

Printed in the USA
CPSIA information can be obtained
at www.ICGtesting.com
LVHW072213031123
762998LV00013B/743